Diplopic

By the same author

Diplopic

Peter Reading

Secker & Warburg
London

First published in England 1983 by
Martin Secker & Warburg Limited
54 Poland Street, London W1V 3DF
Reprinted 1983
Copyright © Peter Reading 1983

British Library Cataloguing in Publication Data

Reading, Peter
  Diplopic.
  I. Title
  821' .914   PR6068. E27

  ISBN 0-436-40983-6

Printed in Great Britain by
Antony Rowe Ltd.
Chippenham

291201

Contents

Acknowledgements

Some of these poems have previously appeared in *Ambit, Encounter, Here Now,* the *Literary Review,* the *Poetry Book Society Supplement 1982, Poetry Durham, Poetry Review* and the *Times Literary Supplement* or been broadcast by the BBC.

The author is grateful to the Arts Council of Great Britain and Sunderland Polytechnic who awarded him a Fellowship from 1981-83, and his personal thanks are due to John Coggrave and Emrys Hughes.

Optician, I am having Double Visions
to see one thing from two sides. Only
give me a Spectacle and I am delighted.

— English Phrases for Malay Visitors
(Vest-Pocket Editions, 1950)

(1) Vulture, aloof on a thermal;
    frail flesh is a commodity
    to be scavenged.
(2) Vulture, manipulating still-bloody bones
    on the white sand;
    Poet, ordering the words of a beautiful sonnet
    on the bare page.

— Two Visions
(after Kokur Niznegorsky)

Is this Thalia and Melpomene, or am I seein double?

— Eavesdropped
(in a Greek restaurant)

At Marsden Bay

Arid hot desert stretched here in the early
Permian Period — sand dune fossils
are pressed to a brownish bottom stratum.
A tropical saline ocean next silted
calcium and magnesium carbonates
over this bed, forming rough Magnesian
Limestone cliffs on the ledges of which
Rissa tridactyla colonizes —
an estimated four thousand pairs
that shuttle like close-packed tracer bullets
against dark sky between nests and North Sea.
The call is a shrill 'kit-e-wayke, kit-e-wayke',
also a low 'uk-uk-uk' and a plaintive
'ee-e-e-eeh, ee-e-e-eeh'.

Four boys about sixteen years old appear
in Army Stores combat-jackets, one wearing
a Balaclava with long narrow eye-slit
(such as a rapist might find advantageous),
bleached denims rolled up to mid-calf, tall laced boots
with bright polished toe-caps, pates cropped to stubble.
Three of the four are cross-eyed, all are acned.
Communication consists of bellowing
simian ululations between
each other at only a few inches range:
'Gibbo, gerroffotal getcher yaffuga',
also a low 'lookadembastabirdsmon'.

Gibbo grubs up a Magnesian Limestone
chunk and assails the ledges at random,
biffing an incubating kittiwake
full in the sternum — an audible slap.
Wings bent the wrong way, it thumps at the cliff base,
twitching, half closing an eye. Gibbo seizes

a black webbed foot and swings the lump joyously
round and round his head. It emits
a strange wheezing noise. Gibbo's pustular pal
is smacked in the face by the flung poultry, yowls,
and lobs it out into the foam. The four
gambol euphoric like drunk chimps through rock pools.
Nests are dislodged, brown-blotched shells crepitate
exuding thick rich orange embryo goo
under a hail of hurled fossilized desert
two hundred and eighty million years old.

Editorial

Being both *Uncle Chummy's Letter Box*
of *Kiddies' Column* and *Supa Scoop* besides
(Your Headlines As They Happen), and having the shakes
uncellophaning fags this crapulous morning,
I compose: BOY (13) CLUBS DAD TO DEATH,
CHILD (10) SCALDS GRANNY (87) TO DEATH,
SKINHEAD (14) STONES KITTIWAKES TO DEATH
AS RSPCA ASKS 'WHERE'S THE SENSE?'.

Better this afternoon after the Vaults,
I award 50 pence to Adam (9)
for this: 'Dear Uncle Chummy, I am writing
to let you know about my hamster Charlie
who's my best friend . . .' 'Keep up the good work, kiddies . . .'
(sinister dwarfs, next issue's parricides).

Dark Continent

Big fat essays are being inserted
into resistant pigeon-holes. Chalky,
who once lived in Africa, is giving
the SCR the benefit of
his experience in those parts 'The *Nkonga
Herald* often carried reports
of offences of Chicken Buggery . . .'

Flora Mackenzie (2nd Year English)
has tackled, for her Creative Writing,
the sanguinary 'Death of a Grouse'
(*In crumpled feather wings of prayer
Heather she lived in, no man harming
She lies and bleeds her rose red root
Her wattle wilted willed to waste
The bird is free, man's lust is caged . . .*
etcetera, etcetera; God).

'The Prof's in a bit of a sweat. It seems
he picked up the Departmental Phone
and who should be on the other end
but Mrs Mackenzie — gave him pure Hell,
said Flora's run off with a 3rd Year Mining
Engineering student, a black,
one Bongoman Bulawayo, I think,
to Zimbabwe or somewhere, and she said
"Hoots! Toots! What are ye goin to do, mon?"
Prof said "Your daughter *is* over eighteen."
Well, she flew off the handle, said "Hoots! Toots!
I gave her to you in good faith . . ."'

A rose
finger of dawn caresses a mud hut,
awakens the delicate, shy, pale Flora
(who strains and frets under sleek black thew)
to that Dark Continent, where men
are men, and the poultry is very uneasy.

Receipt

Unto the stock, that hath been simmering
slowly for nearly twenty-four hours already,
cast ye a bushel of the following, mixed:
shoots of the sacred Ashphodeliaboo,
Roogin, Wormwillow, Auberjelly Lime,
Elephant Quince, Sweet Portalooforago,
Smiley Potatoes, Voodoo Saxifrapple,
verdant Aspariagora, Zulu Froom,
Lily of fragrant Umpo, Virgin's Ice,
a stick of Popgo (black), two sprigs of Kak-Kak.
Marinade dugs, sliced thickly into steaks,
with Shamilee and crushed dried seeds of Xeppit
    (which method served to cook the white poetess
    Flora, 9th wife of the gourmand Bongoman).

The Terrestrial Globe

Señor Garcia
descends a staircase
hopping on one hand.
Three steps down,
not unnaturally,
he sprains his wrist
and sprawls in the sawdust.
He leaps to his feet,
bows, bursts into tears.

Il Maestro subdues
two lionesses,
two Bengal tigresses
and one unidentified
heavily moulting
very male quadruped.

The Brothers Alfonso
perform on stilts.
One of them bears
a striking likeness
to *Señor Garcia*
and, trying to do
'The very difficult
Backward Somersault',
falls on his head.
He removes his stilts,
bows, bursts into tears.

'And now, all the way
from West Germany,'
(a bald Chinese
of ferocious aspect
and droopy moustaches

flexes her biceps)
'The Strongest Woman
The World Has Known,
Miss Herculess,
will carry *Miss Jill*
in this gigantic
Terrestrial Globe.'
Miss Jill climbs into
the ferrous contraption,
sealed in tight
with a saucer-like lid.
The Chinese raises
the huge sphere until
it is over her head
then hurls it clanging
into the ground.
The audience gasps,
screams come from within.
Anxious hands drag
Miss Jill out to safety,
blood smears her costume.
Miss Herculess shrieks,
first in Cantonese,
then in thick Glaswegian,
'D'ye ken I'm no blind!
Keep awa frae my mon!'

A dromedary
of prodigious age
is chased by two llamas
gratuitously
round several dozen
laps of the Big Top . . .

The big cats

       bicker. Fodens churn the rec.
into an Auerbach slough. A squat grey bomb
of Calor hisses under a caravan
labelled not only JILL – CONTORTIONIST

but also SEÑOR GARCIA – FABULOUS
MANIPULATOR EXTRAORDINAIRE
and also THE STRONGEST WOMAN KNOWN TO MAN.
Two tigresses tease red skin, suck stiff bone.

Grunts, lately of the jungle, fade to moans.
The lettered van jolts on its springs. Pink bare
meat rises slowly in the steamed-up glass.
Glut, guzzle, slurp, drool, slobber, mumble, snort –

rank felines, scarcely tame, extravasate,
vie to possess inflamed raw purple flesh.

Minima

After

     the telegram-boy's purse-lipped dirge,
the slicing open,
the ghastly revelation,

the bereaved Parnassian
hones a canine tooth,
sharpens a pencil.

Epicedium

Ah well, it could be worse — it could be *me*.

Telecommunication

The telegram-boy's little red Suzuki.
The pasted strips TELEPHONE FATHER URGENT.
The feeling trembly, squittery and pukey.
The breakfast things left in the cold detergent.
The milled edge of a coin on the thumb-pad.
The voice at the other end 'Yes, late last night'.
The feeling scared/exhilarated/numb. Sad
memories of — (enough of all that shite).

The puny hug, meant to propitiate.
Strong, palliating Fino de Jerez.
The weak reply, meant to initiate
a five-year-old into peculiar Death
'Yes, Grandma's bones *might* fossilize, of course,
like those in your *First Book of Dinosaurs*'.

War Artistes

(There is one of them War Artistes with our lot. He seems not quite human. He drawers even when the heavy firing is on. He done a water colours picture of poor Carew with his head blowed clean off — a very pretty thing, and I don't think! I think he SEES things different to us. — From a letter to his brother, c. 1917, by Thomas Gibb, in the author's possession.)

We are always out there
     with pencils raised,
treacherous bastards,
     Double Agents
not working for *you*
     but for some Secret Power.

If an awful thing happens,
     we will appear —
coyotes, dingoes,
     jackals, hyenas,
lapping up
     universal holocausts.

We have a horrible
     kind of diplopia —
(1) straight, clinical,
     accurate, X-ray,
(2) refracted
     to serve our bent calling.

Mnemonics

Some matter is too delicate to define
with muted chalks or the restricted palette
implicit in small portable tubes of gouache
(e.g. the whitish-tallows and wax-yellows
and algal-greens of military flesh).
Mnemonics are essential — the best method
is to annotate draft studies in the field
for later more urbane studio finish.

May in the squares is the white of Devon cream,
in the warm sun ripe Georgian brick assumes
the russet of port half a century old.
Ribs bright cream, whitest teeth . . . wrote Kennington
on his dead Jerry (circa 1916)
that hangs now in peaceful Clifford Street, West One.

P.S.

The stitching new on your tiny rectangle of black,
you immerse yourself in the sad therapy of the kitchen,
withdrawing from sight when assailed by trembling and weeping.
I mailed you my useless sympathy but, reticently,
withheld admiration and love for you (old-fashioned words)
who, having a grim chore to finish, get on with the job.

Hints

Find ways to make the narrative compel,
I advise students; as, in retailing this,
you might lend the issue added poignancy
by being distanced — describe the electrified
overgrown line in cool botanical terms,
white cow-parsley, *Anthriscus sylvestris,*
adding the child with anthropological
detachment, ten years old, print dress, bewildered . . .

Compelling, maybe, but mere narrative —
no moral or intellectual envoy.
Accentuate the dignified resilience
that humans, or some, are capable of still,
evinced in the sad braveness of the bereaved
whose daughter, being blind, observed no warning.

At Home

She is nearly 87,
and her house is ten years older.
In the garden huge old beech trees,
silver-boled in winter sunshine,
have the following carved on them
(though the scars are mossed and healed now):
JOHN CAREW L SALLY HIBBERT.
In her chair of woven basket,
in the window-bay with pot-plants,
she drinks Earl Grey every morning,
reads the *Telegraph* and wonders
why young people now are vicious,
disrespectful, stoned and randy.
On her knees a tartan blanket,
in her lap soft-centre bon-bons.
(An interior like that in
Lamb's *Portrait of Lytton Strachey.)*

In a silver cage a mynah
chews a grape and spits the pips out.
In a silver frame a photo
of a young World War I soldier
signed JC in faded sepia.

Carved black elephants, brass kettles
fitted with bright amber handles,
Taj Mahals by moonlight rendered
in bright dyes on thin silk, jewel-
hilted daggers indicate some
past connection with the raj. Dates
gleam in chevrons down a central
spine in a round-ended carton.

* * *

Senior Police Officials
dealing with the case were 'frankly
baffled' as to who could do this.
Supa Scoop's reporter comments:

>   This is no mere petty break-in.
>   Here was a defenceless woman,
>   frail, old, well-liked, partly crippled,
>   living on her Old Age Pension,
>   living all alone, her only
>   company an ageing cage-bird,
>   scalded, beaten, slashed, hair pulled out,
>   fingers broken — her assailants
>   making off (when, quite unable
>   to supply them information
>   as to any 'hoard of savings',
>   she fell at their feet unconscious),
>   making off with £1.60,
>   making off with *£1.60,*
>   *making off with £1.60*
>   and a box of CHOCKO YUM-YUMS.

* * *

In the tray of sand and faeces
at the bottom of the bird-cage
it spins rhythmically on one wing
where a stump of singed flight-feathers
joins a dislocated shoulder.
All the primaries are burnt off.
It emits a hissing whisper
'Hello sailor. Hello sailor.'
Slowly, nictitating membranes
squeeze across dull-bloomed sclerotics.

* * *

When she opened up the front door
Gibbo punched her in the guts like,
give her head-butts, dragged her screamin
into the front room. I says 'Look,
where's yer bleedin money, Mrs?'
She says nuffink so I rubs these
chocolates what she had hard in her
face like. Then we gets this knife thing
what she had hung on the wall like
and we gives her face the old quick
criss-cross with the point. She give us
all this crap: 'Wah-wah, you demons,
have you no love for your mothers?'
So I gives her hair a bleedin
pull what sent her screamin. It was
dead great, how she screamed and screamed and
how her hair come out in handfuls.
Gibbo gets this bleedin budgie
what she had in this big cage thing
and he got its wings and lit them
with his old fag-lighter. It was
dead great how that parrot-thing went
up in smoke. Gib bit its beak off.
That was dead great, how he done it.
Then we found her purse and all it
had was bleedin one pound fifty
so we give her fingers the old
snap-snap like and Gibbo tells her
'If you don't say where you've got it
hid, I'll give ya boilin water.'
An he did. That was dead great like.
There was dates — I don't like them much.

Mynah Petrarchan*

What a big fellow *he* is for his age!
Give us a drink. I likes a drop of rum.
Hello there, sailor boy! Who loves his mum?
Look at that bird! Let's stuff it full of sage
and onion! Cocky's out on the rampage!
Everyone loves black Cocky! Give us some!
Cocky's a wicked naughty! Smack his bum!
Cocky likes nice boys. Lock him in his cage.

Cocky must stay inside. Sit on his perch.
Speak to me, Cocky. Say a little wordie.
Give us a kiss, then. Who's a pretty boy?
What would poor mummy do left in the lurch?
What if the bad boys got her little birdie?
Where would she be without her pride and joy?

*Declaimed by Oriental passerine.

After Sanraku Koshu

Jailed for being drunk,
but far from contrite, the bard,
minus shoes, tie, belt,
savoured steel grille, rank pallet,
mused 'Ah! Raw Material!'

Sortie

'Didn't you hear about it? Well, as planned, he
went up to Town and lunched quite well at Wheeler's
— Pol Roger '71 with half a dozen
large Irish oysters, fine bottle of Clicquot
'75 with a dressed lobster, '60
Dow's with a Stilton. Looked up "Stinker"'s cousin,
drank '63 Warre's with him at the Savile,
then on to "Stinker"'s for Cockburn's '45.
Caught, by mistake, a train to Crewe, where Peelers
found him in deep repose (fatigued by travel
and tiny phials of Inter-City brandy).
Night spent in durance vile. Next day the Beak — "Oh,
tell me, are you drunk frequently?". He fixed the
ass with a scowl and got quite haughty — "I've
never touched Strong Drink (but for a Christmas Fino)."
£10. Quite an amusing little beano.'

15th February

I tried to put in what I really felt.
I really tried to put in what I felt.
I really felt it — what I tried to put.
I put it really feelingly, or tried.
I felt I really tried to put it in.
What I put in I tried to really feel.
Really I felt I'd tried to put it in.
I really tried to feel what I put in.

It cost £5 in WH Smith's.
£5 it cost — WH Smith's ain't cheap.
£5 ain't cheap, not for a thing like that.
It costs, a thing like that — £5 ain't cheap.
It wasn't a cheap thing — £5 it cost.
A thing like that ain't cheap in WH Smith's.
In WH Smith's a thing like that comes costly.
A lot to pay, £5, for a thing like that.

The heart was scarlet satin, sort of stuffed.
I sort of felt it was me own heart, like.
SHE TORE THE STUFFING OUT OF THE SCARLET HEART.
I sort of stuffed and tore her sort of scarlet.
I stuffed her, like, and felt her sort of satin.
I sort of felt she'd tore out all me stuffing.
I felt her stuff like satin sort of scarlet
her stuff felt sore, torn satin whorlet scar
I liked her score felt stiffed her scar lick hurt
I tore her satin felt her stuffed her scarlet
tore out her heart stuff scarred her Satan har
I licked her stiff tore scarf her harlot hair
tied scarf tore stabbed scar whore sin sat tit star
stuffed finger scar ha ha ha ha ha ha
felt stiff scarf tight tore scarlet heart her scare
her scare stare stabbed heart scarlet feel torn mur

Found

Strange find — a plastic dummy from a boutique
(boots, white long thighs, pants pulled right down, a sack
over the head and torso) dumped among bins
and tumps of fetid garbage and coils of rank
sloppy dog faeces in an ill-lit alley
between the Laundereite and Indian Grocer.
Incorrect diagnosis: it emits
a high-pitched rattle like Callas gargling.

Rescrutinizing 36 hours later:
what was, in sodium light, viridian,
is, in pale February sun, maroon.
About a soup-cupful remains still viscous,
black at the rim where a scabbed mongrel sniffs,
ripples taut sinew, salivates and laps.

Stedman's

I am going to write a sonnet
concerning Huntington's Chorea
from the viewpoint of a Year 2
Pharmacy student, and so
I am looking up **Chorea** in
Stedman's Medical Dictionary.

On the same page as I require,
this appears: **Choreophrasia** —
The continual repetition
of meaningless phrases.

                    I wonder
if I ought, after all, to dispatch
the pharmacist's Granny by means of
convulsions, or whether to have her
reduced to a jabbering night-hag
whose terminal speech* could be rendered
with agreeable anarchy.

---

*   Carew, Carew, Carew, my bonny lad.
Where do we go from here? Brisk cockatoo.
Happy the man who knows not he is glue.
Which way? Which way? I *love* Jahanabad
in Spring. What drunken bard? An ironclad
means tank. My bonny lad. Carew, Carew.
From here we venture to the Portaloo
of death. Brisk cockatoo is very bad!
      I had a Polly budgie in a box.
Seagull and fox. Paisley is *not* OK.
Carew, Carew, Carew, cock, cocky, cocky.
These sweets are jolly fudgy. Chicken Pox!
These literary magazines are fey,
cock, cocky, cock. Carew. I hates a trochee!

In *A Sort of Life,* Greene remarked
(mitigating the relish with which
he observed parental distress
at the death of a ten-year-old)
'There is a splinter of ice
in the heart of a writer.'

                        I savour
the respective merits of one
kind of mayhem over another,
contentedly ponder the species
of fourteen-liner most apposite —
Petrarchan? Elizabethan?

A Recollection

She always was a great one for the pranks.
We hadn't seen her for about 5 years.
To find her in that place with all those cranks
was like one of her jokes — we laughed till our tears
unfocused her as she winked, twitched and flexed
her limbs. Then we saw that she was weeping too,
realized the reason for the high-walled, annexed,
discreetly-labelled building.

                               Sleeping through
most of the morning's 2nd Year Pharmacy,
he emerged drowsily, heard, as in a dream,
'. . . Huntington's Chorea. Though, when calmer, she
exhibited no more symptoms than extreme
involuntary twitching . . .' and recalled
the childhood visit and was newly appalled.

Nips

Look at the high tor!
The rocks are older than men
and will last longer.

Thank you very much
for pointing this out to us,
PBS Spring Choice.

* * *

Crossing the campus
with a 6 by 6 canvas
in a force 7,
the art student looks like a
discomfited Wright brother.

His large oil depicts
a seagull in a tweed suit
boxing with a fox
who wears muffler and flat cap.
(An allegory, I think.)

* * *

Touching to see men
normally at variance
unite (in whining
about meagre salaries
at the Faculty Meeting).

* * *

The Prime Minister
is an incompetent fool,
Rustics are bumpkins,
Townies are corrupt. I am
a good man and know what's what.

* * *

In last week's press, X
reviewed Y: *One of the best
poets now writing.*

In this week's press, Y
reviews X: *One of the best
poets writing now.*

* * *

Not Nell Gwynn (alas),
but the <u>intense</u>, short, hirsute
editor of *Stand*
importunes our theatre queue —
'Come! Buy my juicy lit. mags!'

Phoney-rustic bards,
spare us your thoughts about birds,
butterflies, fish, snakes
and mammals (including us)
— biologists write more sense.
Down the lab they think
these crows, peasants, pikes, eels, swifts
are twee, ill-observed.

Bumpkins, from whose bums
you consider the sun shines,
think you're townee twits.
Like that haiku frog,
unscientific fauna
is a bore in verse.

Ex Lab

I

Dilute acetic
has exposed from the matrix
(limestone, Jurassic),
ischium and ilium
and interlocking pubis.

These demonstrate how
ornithischian hip-joints
differ from those of
saurischians. These bits are
believed. *Scelidosaurus.*

After coffee-break
they will be made ready for
hardening resin.
                 These flimsy inked surfaces
                 come from the Late Holocene:

                 CIRCUS STRONG-WOMAN
                 CONVICTED OF MANSLAUGHTER.
                 STUDENT 'GOES MISSING'
                 IN AFRICAN MYSTERY.
                 SKINHEAD SETS FIRE TO CAGE-BIRD.

In what was Dorset
one hundred and eighty five
million years ago,
Megalosaurus et al
flenched, flensed these bastards to mince.

II

I am cleaning up
a piece of dinosaur shit
(Upper Cretacious,
length 20 centimetres)
that came from Mongolia.

Someone else requires
the air-abrasive machine
urgently. I stop
and peruse my copy of
a Nietzsche biography.

> Up to a point, yes.
> 'God is dead' — quite straightforward.
> But why, then, go on
> to think some mitigation
> is needed for us to face
>
> Godless cosmic dust?
> Matter just gets on with it.
> Saying 'YES to life',
> conceiving 'Übermenschen'
> is an arrogant sell-out
>
> quite as fey as 'God'.
> Anyway, Nietzsche was nuts —
> got stopped by the fuzz
> for taking off his clothing
> and bathing in a puddle.

This one matrix holds
fragments of eggshell (believed
Protoceratops —
about ninety million years
of age) and a turd fossil.

I believe in this:
no Übermenschen's remnant
(not one coprolite)
is going to be better
than this elegant stone crap.

III

       Is Sin Sinful*ness?*
       preoccupies my pious
       colleagues over lunch.
Hydrogen and Helium —
the Original Sinners.

On this diagram
(chrono-stratigraphical),
3.6 billion
years ago may be seen as
about the start of Earth life.

       When your daughter dies
       aged ten, mown down by a train,
       console yourself thus:
       sky-pilots can forgive her
       by saying a Special Thing.

On this diagram,
the Holocene or Recent
(last ten thousand years)
is far, far, far, far too small
to register on this scale.

> You live, then you die.
> This is extremely simple.
> You live, then you die —
> no need to wear funny hats,
> no need for mumbo-jumbo.

IV

The '62 find,
Heterodontosaurus
(southern Africa,
Upper Trias), concerned me
greatly because of the *teeth*

(rather than because
Scelidosaurus had been
the earliest known
ornithischian till then)
— that almost 'canine' 'eye-tooth'!

> Oozing bonhomie,
> we take unwanted nick-nacks
> to the Oxfam shop —
> at last! the starving millions
> will have a nice bite to eat!

The stomach contents
of an *Anatosaurus*
I am working on
were mummified — pine-needles
seventy million years old.

       In Belfast, I read,
       the craze is for hunger-strikes.
       Eat your porridge up
       like good little murderers
       (Political Status, balls).

These five gastroliths
(stomach-stones to grind food) were
worn smooth as pool balls
by an unknown sauropod
of the Upper Jurassic.

Called to specialize
in one stratigraphical
field, I decided
the Late Holocene (*our* scene)
did not concern me greatly.

V

At the end of the
Cretacious, a 'Great Dying'
seems to have occurred,
when half of all animal
and plant groups became extinct.

That extinction seems
to have been protracted for
a few million years;
this one, now underway, will
have reached a similar scale

in a few decades.
The hiatus resulting
in some processes
of evolution will be
extremely fascinating.

      'SUPER-TANKA SINKS'
      (the mis-print suggests Baroque,
      fugal, cumbersome
      development of the Five-
      Seven-Five-Seven-Seven . . .).

What one enjoys most
is the manipulation
of these hapless things
at such impartial distance
to fit an imposed order.

Of course one does not
really care for the *objects,*
just the *subject.* It
is a Vulture Industry,
cashing-in on the corpses.

Vacuum, cosmic dust,
algae, rhipidistians,
internecine us
(it is a fucking good job
that it all does not matter).

From a Journal (c. 1917, in the author's possession)

My Grandfather knew Gideon Algernon Mantell
(discoverer of the Iguanodon)
who shewed him, in 1822, in Sussex,
those teeth! of creatures hitherto undreamed-of.

My Grandfather, in 1841,
was at the B.A.A.S. Plymouth meeting*
when Doctor (later Prof., Sir) Richard Owen
unleashed the Dinosaur on smug Victorians.

My Grandfather, a polymath, drew well,
botanized, 'Englished' Vergil, geologized.
My Grandfather was born in 1800,
Father in 1850, I myself
in 1895 . . .

       He would have been
88 (but for 1917).

---

*At the 1841 Plymouth meeting of the British Association
for the Advancement of Science, Owen (1804-1892), first
Director of the Natural History Museum in South Kensington,
suggested that *Iguanodon*, *Megalosaurus* and *Hylaeosaurus*
should together be named the Dinosauria, the 'terrible
lizards'.

Englished (ii. 458)

Far from the clash of Celt twerps,
        the Barley Mow telly transmits
atrocities none of the rustics
        attends to lest they eclipse
his own catalogue of woes —
        the price of bag-muck increases,
Hill Subsidies insufficient
        to run the Merc and the Rover.

The muggings, the dole queues, the miners
        (audaciously asking for more)
are ignored; the new Combine is costing
        (Nat-West) 46 grand,
masonry bees are molesting
        the Georgian brick of the Glebe.
Salopian swains make merry
        with rough rhymes and boisterous mirth.

O fortunatos nimium,
        sua si bona norint . . .
— farmers are fortunate fuckers,
        wanting the wit to know it.

(Shropshire, July 1981)

Englished (iii. 349-83)

Winter is simply beastly for northern neatherds,
girt in the smelly pelts of Reynard and Ursa,
crouched in uncomfy igloos killing time swilling
gassy cyder and frothy Bass and frolicking.

Boreas's eastern child whines incessantly.
You could drive your muck-spreader on the icèd tarn.
The kine are all dead and under 7 cubits
of snow. The antlery tribes are stuck numb in drifts.

Your duds freeze stiff as you stand by the elm log blaze.
Brazen nick-nacks from Brum burst asunder with cold.
Icicles crackle in uncombed hairies' beavers.
It's really really rotten to be Rhyphaean.

Oenophiles give you Grands Crus by weight, not volume,
cleaving the frozen Lafite with their tomahawks.

(Tyne & Wear, January 1982)

Epithalamium

I

. . . have great pleasure in . . .
of their daughter Crystal . . .
enclosed Gift List . . .

Dragonstraw door mat in plaited seagrass
from China.
'Tik Tok' wall clock, battery operated
quartz movement in pine frame.
'La Primula Stripe' dishwasher-proof
glazed earthenware coffee set.
Valance with neat box pleats to fit
3ft to 5ft beds (fixed by Velcro pads).
Michel Guérard's kitchen work table
with base of solid pine, including
a duckboard shelf for storage,
a knife rack and pegs for teacloths.
Boxwood pastry crimper.
'Confucius' 50% polyester,
50% cotton duvet cover.
Pine wine rack.
Pine lavatory paper holder.
Solid pine toilet seat with chrome fittings
(coated with 6 layers of polyurethane).
Iron omelette pan with curved sides.
Angus Broiler cast iron pan for steaks
and chops which combines the ease of frying
with the goodness of grilling.
'Leonardo' sofa in cream herringbone.
Honey-coloured beech bentwood rocker
with cane back and seat.
Cork ice-bucket with aluminium insert.
'Mr Toad' rattan chair from France.
Tough cotton canvas Sagbag filled
with flame-retardant polystyrene granules.

II

The fizz is Spanish, labelled 'MEGOD CHAMPAIN'.

III

. . . have great pleasure in . . .
will now read Greetings Cards . . .

    de da de da de da de da this wedding gift to you
    de da de da de da de da your golden years come true . . .
    All the way from America . . .
    sorry can't be there . . .
    would love to have been there . . .
    a California 'Howdy!' . . .
    de da de da de da de da all your hopes and fears
    de da de da de da de da throughout the coming years . . .
    have made their bed, must *lay* in it . . .

HA HA HA HA HA HA HA (what a riot the Best Man *is*).

IV

At their new home — 'Crimmond' (next to 'Sinatra' on one side
and 'Mon Rêve' on the other) — the presents are laid out.
They look lovely, don't they, Confucius, Leonardo and Mr Toad.

V

Bog paper and boots are tied to their bumper.
Consummation in Calais is nothing to write home about.

Carte Postale

Dear Mum and Dad,
                    The picture shows a 'gendarme'
which means policeman. France is overrated.
For two weeks it has been wet. 9th September:
we had a 'dégustation' in the Côte
de Mâconnais and Mal got quite light-headed.
Sometimes I think it will be *too* ideal
living with Mal — it's certainly the Real
Thing. I must go now — here comes Mal.
                                        Love, Crystal.

Encircling her slim waist with a fond arm,
the husband of a fortnight nibbles her throat,
would be dismayed to learn how she had hated
that first night when in Calais he had kissed all
over her, and, oh God!, how she now dreaded
each night the importunate mauve-capped swollen member.

Between the Headlines

(Not if she knew her X-ray result.)
STAR QUITS HOSPITAL CURED

(Not acrimonious veg
but internecine Celts.)
GREENS CLASH WITH ORANGES

*(Not like a mongrel picking up spare bones,
I try to photograph wars with compassion*
opines McCullin* on purveying mayhem.)
BABY SHOT IN BELLY

(Not democratic: on Election Day,
soldiers, the oldest of them about 15,
dispose of corpses at the polling booths
then resume licking their lollipops.)
30,000 CIVILIANS CLAIMED

(Not nice Nips send huge
vessel containing crude-oil
to drive imported
Yamahas and Suzukis
and bugger up your beaches.)
SUPER-TANKA SINKS – SLICK SLAYS SEAGULLS

(Not had such a supper in their life
and the little ones chewed on the bones-o
bones-o
bones-o
not had such a supper in their life
and the little ones chewed on the bones-o.)
STUDENT 'GOES MISSING' IN AFRICAN MYSTERY

---

*Declared by *Newsweek* 'the greatest battlefield photographer of our time'.

(Not-Foreskin v Foreskin —
Old Testament berks
in daft dressing-gowns
and peep-toe slippers
play atavistic
grenade-lobbing pranks
in the Holy Land.)

SALAAM/SHALOM SHAM

(Not to be regarded
as more than a physiological
characteristic — a big brain
does not mean specific aloofness.
Don't think *thinking* makes you
different from, say, rhipidistians.
Souls/arse-holes are the same stuff
— very thin stripes in a tall cliff.)

PORTALOO CLAIMS FOSSIL PROF

Admissions

Both were unconscious on arrival, one
with serious head injuries, the other
with broken back and ribs and damaged pelvis
(they were put with the factory accident
who'd been admitted earlier with a severed
arm, only 16, he died later too).
Both had been injured when a lorry shed
its load of Portaloo site-lavatories
impartially on a bus queue. One of them,
a circus tightrope-walker, sat bolt upright,
bowed, burst into floods of tears and then expired
wheezing 'Miss Jill! Miss Jill! Miss Jill!'. The other,
a palaeontologist, died screaming out
'THE HOLOCENE DID NOT CONCERN ME GREATLY!'.

Finds

I

The *Mammuthus,* winched from the permafrost
during the famous Schmitstein expedition
of '51, was truly magnificent,
the finest-preserved specimen yet found —
tusks 4.8 m, 3.3 at shoulder.

It was transported, carefully supervised
by scientists from the Ghustphsen Institute,
back to the base at Skruskhev where impromptu
laboratory facilities were installed.

One of the expedition's porters owned
a husky of unprepossessing aspect.
One night it gained admission to the lab
and ate the 20,000 year-old trunk.

II

The Schneider had one 75 mm
gun, also two machine guns. Double armour
plates on the front, the sides and top. These plates
were separated with a 1.5
inch space between them. Armour varied from
.2 inches to .95 inches.
Maximum speed about 5 miles per hour.
Vertical coil springs, jointed bogie frames.
Tracks — solid plates with single grousers, width
was 14 inches, pitch 10 inches. Length
19 feet 8, width 6 feet 7, height
7 feet 10. Weight 14.9 tons.
A Schneider 70 horse-power water-cooled
4 cylinder engine. There were sliding gears,

3 forward, 1 reverse. Range — 25
miles on a fuel tank holding 53
gallons. Equipped with double tailpiece. Nose
intended as wire-cutter and to assist
in crossing obstacles. Unditching beam
carried on right side. Dome ventilating louvre
on top of hull. The overhanging hull
greatly reduced rough-ground mobility.
Vertical armour plates could not withstand
the celebrated German bullet the 'K'.

A nasty versifier is researching,
sniffing historic carnage, adding salt . . .

Resolution

When the French tank the *Schneider* was introduced
(capable of 6 kilometres per hour,
weight 15 tons, guns 75 mm)
in the bright April sun of '17,
a subaltern watched two tree-pipits ascend
from the black jagged shelled limbs of a pine
and entered sundry commonplaces in this
journal — concluding with the desultory

Watched pipits' song-flight. Saw new ironclad
capable of 6 kilometres per hour,
weight 15 tons, guns 75 mm.
Tonight, after lights-out, I am resolved,
although I love you, Sally, to lie brow-down
on a grenade and then to detonate it.

Tryst

Me and Gib likes it here — always comes of a night,
no one else gets here, see. That's his Great-Grandad's stone.
Gassed, *he* was; got sent home from one of them *old* wars.
   Tommy, they called him.

We sprayed HARTLEPOOL WANKERS on one of them. Great!
This is the newest one — sad it is, really, it's
some little ten-year-old girlie's. Them plastic daffs
   look very nice, though.

He likes to get me down in the long weeds between
two of them marble things — I can see ivy sprout
on the cross by his head. He makes me squiggle when
   he sticks his hand up.

He works at one of them mills what makes cattle food.
He stacks the sacks. You should see them tattoos on his
arms when he flexes them. There is a big red heart
   with TRUE LOVE on it.

He runs the Packer-thing all on his own, he does.
We're saving up to get married and have a big
do like that big snob that works in our office had
   (Crystal, her name is).

I let him do what he wants — he pretends that he's
the Ripper, sometimes, and gets me down on a grave;
then what he does with his hands feels like scurrying
   rats up my T-shirt.

When we've saved up enough, we're going to wed in church.
This is alright, though — at least in the summertime.
They don't pay poor Gib much, stacking them heavy sacks
   off the conveyor.

Pacepacker

THE *PACEPACKER* NEEDS ONE OPERATOR ONLY.
PLACE EMPTY PAPER SACKS IN RACK MARKED 'SACKS',
ENSURING THEY ARE CLAMPED TIGHT WITH SPRING CLAMP.
ADJUST CONVEYORS TO CORRECT HEIGHTS. SWITCH ON.
WHEN 'START RUN' LIGHT SHOWS GREEN, PRESS 'START RUN'
                                                    BUTTON.
SACKS ARE PICKED UP BY SUCKERS, STITCHED AND CONVEYED
TO ELEVATOR. ENSURE CLOTHING AND HANDS
ARE CLEAR OF CONVEYOR BELT.

                             The corrugated
rapidly-moving strip of rubber seemed
to draw the arm smoothly, unresistingly
up through the oiled steel rollers. The 'Stop Run' light
shows red. The matt belt glistens where a smear
of pink mulch, fatty lumps, flensed skin, singed hair,
is guzzled dry by plump impartial houseflies.